Maria Grazia Calandrone

FOSSILS

Translated from the Italian
by Johanna Bishop, Barry Callaghan
and Anatoly Kudryavitsky

SurVision Books

First published in 2018 by
SurVision Books
Dublin, Ireland
www.survisionmagazine.com

Copyright © Maria Grazia Calandrone, 2018
Translations © Johanna Bishop, 2018
Translations © Barry Callaghan, 2018
Translations © Anatoly Kudryavitsky, 2018

Design © SurVision Books, 2018

Cover image courtesy of Fossil Butte National Monument, Wyoming, USA.

ISBN: 978-1-9995903-6-9

This book is in copyright. No part of this publication may be reproduced, stored in a retrieval system or transmitted in any form or by any means without the prior permission in writing from the publisher.

Pages 4 to 28 translated by Johanna Bishop.
Pages 29 and 30 translated by Anatoly Kudryavitsky.
Pages 31 to 37 translated by Barry Callaghan.

Acknowledgements

Grateful acknowledgement is made to the editors of the following, in which a number of these poems originally appeared: *Exile, SurVision, OOMPH! Contemporary Works in Translation: A Multilingual Anthology (Vol II)*, Oomph! Press, 2018.

CONTENTS

Travelling Light   4
From "The Disappeared"
  I've Added a Transparent Body to the House   6
  The Altar of the Species   8
  You Won't Have a Life   10
From "On Everyone's Lips"
  Things Out of Sight   11
  A Clear Situation   12
  We Can Imagine It Gleaming in the Morning Light   13
  Invocation for the Coast of Persephone   14
  Children's Song   15
From "Fossils"
  Golden Age   16
  Per alba   17
  Imaginary Letter   18
  Forever forever forever   19
  Garden of Original Joy   20
  Tree, Fossil   23
  Garden of Joy   24
From "Good Morals"
  Incipit   25
From "The Responsible Machine"
  The Great Animal's Apocalypse   27
  Maria, the Apparitions   28
  The World, Exposed   29
  Mosses Pave the Way for Spring   30
  Inside the Crawling Month   31
  The Wind on the Sea Is Scaly Being Prone to Massacre   32
  Said in Symbols   33
  Perhaps It Was the Age, the Circumstance   34
  I Did Not Move Ahead Just Barely...   36

Travelling Light

1. The Sea

The Tyrrhenian is a cage of salt
an ailing corpse
to be mimicked
in the impassive sleep of an animal.

The contortion of the rocks
broken loins of enormous phenomena passing
along the coastal ribs
animals laid out for calm weather.

The saints stood like cormorants
—their beaks bound
to the articulations of the sea
they serve as bellwethers for caravans.

The watershed of summer savory
the recumbent aviary of the mistral—with their tufts
of wings withered one by one, verging on a forest
                              of saline derivation.

The Aeolian peace of the cliffs, vast
battle horns
above the clay flats still as sanctuaries
and mines of salt silver
merchant ships in the bunker of tillage.

2. The Land

A vast winding sheet over the bass drum of the sea
where the inanimate
is at work
and the sea flares toward the unleavened white
of the human flock that apes the dry heat of the
                                seagulls and the herd.

Cows
wheat-coloured
in the melancholy sun—an untamed field
of sweet sweet milk.

Beaches hatched from centuries of mourning, out of kilter
on an earth
left incomplete by the vacant chime of sun and full of
                                lowing.

It can only be holy because on the island all is empty
earth without sight
without the glow of animals
and in the orb of dawn the sad axe
of the wrist
hisses down to the bone of the tree. A cross
of silence bursts out
into the sacred chorus
—into the gleanings
of extinct herbs that taste of crater ash.

From "The Disappeared"

I've Added a Transparent Body to the House

Seeing how he played with the ball and watching the
                            skeletal fluctuation of his
soul in the form of a shadow surrounding its arcs—
                    the red orbits, the belltowers

of the ball over the vast
catalogue of the earth—the girl said to him but then
                                  you're just
like me!: kneeling, simple, struck to the heart—the
                                      way the earth
overflown by darting spheres
reveals your structure as an elevated animal.

But I think that you'll come back
on two legs—because you moved forward (with a bag
that was light, almost empty) constantly towards a
                                      domestic
scale. I
am at peace, given
the light I bend your silence to.
Face-to-face with your silence
I remember, I am consumed by brotherhood
You now are body that I do not see but which
must have been. It is as beautiful as love contemplating
its own account of violence and peace, to know after it's over

that you built the visible and invisible together
like a tower with a tower at the top, the entire factory
of the world

The Altar of the Species

She was easy to love but she was destined
to disappear in haste and yet to make
certain provisions that clues reveal to have been
meticulous. In the afternoon she would tend the garden
silently. We didn't get what she was thinking, she was
so serene. Or else
she would be busy with a notepad. Every night—once the last
                                                            client
got his clothes back on—she'd buy some pastry for her mother's
                                                            breakfast.

Debris floats through the water and is caught
at regular intervals by the grating buried
in the darkness and the silence that form many yards below
the superficially aerial appearance of the water
caused by the sun's dawdling at the summit like a democratic
lacquer, an overflowing gush of optimism
even in the nettlefields deboned by the brunt of the factories.
It is called the hemp mill road and leads
in a mixture of mud and clods
that keeps the animal chaff from sinking in, to the hydroelectric
plant—it is an interrupted sentiment, a drift of continents and
                                        their submerged catastrophes
in the island of the body that ends up
at the door of the housing project: there's just one guard who is
                                                          watching
the to and fro between the two sides of water and serpentine
                                                                 flame
                        or perhaps transmigration.

We find her in a strange state of abandon
as if all her ligaments were cut:
almost none of the canal water
no evil thoughts
no irony
not a drop of water in her lungs, not even
diatomic—her body buoyed up by a critical light
beyond its own abandonment—was pulsing in the sun as if
                                                            in ecstasy.

You Won't Have a Life

The shoes were never found.
But the light beat coitally on the body of the girl
crystallized into evidence.
Between her eyes and womb
traces of the washhouse—working backwards to establish alibis.
The door turned out to be shut and double-locked.

She was burning like a host in the lacrimal
matter of the late afternoon—head caught among the bushes
and the obstinate repeated twists. Due to unknown causes
she did not make it to her birthday
whatever function her years would have had individually but an
                                                                                 immobile
farewell to the beauty of the world
warmed the fibre that endures
joyous cry of the body free from pain.

From "On Everyone's Lips"

Things Out of Sight

As if in ritual binding
these crosses of wheat
unripened
on the body that is also green, incorruptible
inkwell
forged from a metal we dip into
for names, for praises
and is mere matter that we learn to use as song:
                                                             ecce
corpus
meum
in absentia
carnal
exploited in this highest of domains
until it let out droplets
of death and of rebirth
– *quia ad omne supplicium paratum*
est, always in ecstasy – raptus
semper, Our Lady
of Loss, because the song of the dead accumulates
and is a new task—wild
flower and rose
of the everyday.

A Clear Situation

The crushing sweetness of the shoulder blades,
                              the halted percussion
of the muscular harness, the valves
that have finally abandoned her
on the earth, the humble angle her head makes
to hide the smile
on the crude column of her body
says: I've been waiting for you all my life
I saw your life
in my dreams and all of it, night
after night, was smoothed out into forgiveness.
                                      At certain points
when the skyful of wonder overlapped
with the bubble of trees shaken by the full
moon, I would wake up
because of your dreams
and would carry your name like a flag
that rose up from my chest and made me
invisible: all of me
that one could see was your name. I knew
that at the close we would be close
whatever else happened to us in the meantime. Now
here I am, I am here to end
in your ending, to breathe in your last breath
from your mouth
and blow it through my mouth
that no one has ever kissed again since you,
to the sky.

We Can Imagine It Gleaming in the Morning Light

For the white soul that holds us up and the romantic roses
for what slowly decays
and breaks off its apparent sleep
among the green handfuls of sun
for this angel with golden heels
that takes on the flavour
of the reservoirs
—of the mills
and of the woodsheds
in the smoke that rises from the excavated earth
as it feels discontent arrive
and endures the same
mysterious smile
of fruitbearing plants
for the firewood that carries contagion
through the rows
divert us from the fact of death:
the body is nothing
thinking of the infinite,
apple tree in the sun
pouring itself out on the heart of the earth
moving free
with the oxide of branches,
the rust
and the sturdy matter
of insects with glowing immortal bodies.

Invocation for the Coast of Persephone

At its maximum point of expansion the trunk
sings like a harmonium
the ducts contract inside
to modulate the song of the species. Turn upside down
in the water to touch the ground and bob
up again two or three times to the surface making
amphibian movements, taking on
the arctic, mercurial colour of amphibians—the pose
of zero, of lack
of interest: only
thus will you pass with your whole body
from realm to realm.
From the shore, among the brown agaves
they will believe in an occupation
of sun in the veins before the eyes of all—
the brotherhood will make them smile.

Children's Song

The air, the first air
you breathed, was the air of March and morning. The sun
burned calmly in its wave
from the window that was wide because wide was
the heart
and disinterested
as the sun that sets its light down on the river water
and sails clear
to the sea
where the space is all riddled
by seagull whistles and nothing
hurts any more. It is beautiful to hold
the new air on the face of the newborn, with hands
that are human hold
sacred the sacred, make the air clearer where it touches
the heart, so that the heart is simple and weightless
as a kite
and other things that move from earth to sky.
It is beautiful to say I will do what I can
and more than myself, like all the other women on the
                                      earth: take, life
from my life
your innocent freedom.

From "Fossils"

Golden Age

I mean when, from too much joy
at being loved, we fall
to earth oh! living flesh
that will lose your voice
in weeping, I mean when
inspired, we build the scenery with hammer and nails
and the fossil of an angel lifts
its wings out of the plaster
of the walls, in the background. I mean when
I embraced all of life in you: both yours
and mine, shining and linked by a prehistoric joy
in the night, which came down from the west
over the countryside. I mean when
you became a virgin again for me
in a transparent hemorrhage of light – oh! such
an extraordinary thing
of an ordinary nature – oh! life
all intact, all
disarrayed, before love
cleanses
it all, back with
it all, this whole life

Per alba

my dear heart is a human god,
                                    a bird from the highlands

nesting night after night in the pale glow
of your breast
like a perfect hendecasyllable verse

                (soul-thing) white and so lavish, slight of wing – rose
                              and bramble, ashes – *parva*
                          among squandered stars,
                                      white blood
of a tube sponge
in the white planetarium, white tiger
sitting by the side of the white painless road

my dear heart grows from your bones
like a rose from a living tongue
        – in drips,
                in a hemorrhage
                        – from your alphabet

beyond picturing
but it is from this body,
from its silent harvest
that the word comes,
this absolute bread
I offer, this beauty so
vivid, made for you

Imaginary Letter

Where I was flesh she was ivory
        —Pier Paolo Pasolini

the dawn
of tender
flesh, trapped
in the exoskeleton of the Law

in the tragic
month of November
everything was weeping

hold me tight, outside
of human bounds

hold me like a mother
in a dreamt embrace

Forever forever forever...

I wish you would put on that dress
you bought on a day in July
after saying I love you too

I wish you would put on that dress
for me, one last time,

then, I wish I could melt into the earth
and rest where she rests

Garden of Original Joy

your flesh blossoming like a flame in the green
                               flame of the country
I don't believe my eyes

I see the golden bronze
of your body coming closer
I don't believe my eyes

you pull volatile gold
out of your chest that can feel love and you tell me
                             between kisses *it's a miracle*
I don't believe my eyes

all the grass and the whole scent of the
                               countryside are awe

this bread left in the grass is awe and awe is the
                       bottle foaming over the flowers

don't wipe your mouth
your beauty has no barriers

my blood contains space without dominion, and
           from the center of all life spills an embrace
                             big as the world

I already told you
back in the city, remember? *look, the world is so big,*
            it's your love that has made room for itself

half-naked, towel over your shoulder
you walk
with flesh reborn out of my kisses

with the feet of a child
you climb the stairs,
you climb up to feel where the soul of a living
                                      creature begins

in the crucial place
there is a vast silence
and a buzzing of mosquitos
the gold of your lips
the white fluttering of your blood

out of the beloved body rises
a glow that pours out,
your whole body making a sound of sea
how your heart beats
and in my blood the same light shines

now and then we laugh at my anguish
that no bigger words exist

if I could open my chest, remember?

I can make up the words
I can make up the whole world
to make you happy

then, I let you go like you wanted

don't go, I said, I miss
what I am with you, this ample
thing, this sun-filled space that becomes what's
                                      good for you

it wasn't the muscle alone that suffered, the whole area
around it ached
and the silence scraped like a rasp and completed
                          the spontaneous work of pain

which echo, what moon, what soil, what crater, which
among the high stars of the night that lit up your
                                 mouth still
happy with love, what pitying planet
was moved to compassion? what was merciful?

your ancestral body has released its astral body

dawn hovering over mortal things when they awake
as if they did not have to die
this is what I know of love: the wounds that take
                                 years to turn back
into flesh that still wants to be blessed with kisses,
                              never leave her alone

Tree, Fossil

you will be fed
at length, further on
in the time of life, by the fruit
of a prehistoric apple tree. in a future April, you
                                        will rise up
with your spine spurred
by new sap,
you will remember the sweetness of the tree that
  would not die and resprouted and reblossomed,
  every time
you cut it. you will turn
back, stretch out your hand, the lovely hand that
                                 so sweetly caressed
the open branches of the apple tree
and you will eat. then I will come back into your
                            mouth gently as light. and again,
in the white heat of our summer time, you will eat
the apple you fished
out of the depths of time, the fruit red and swollen
as an artery, running
from my life to your life,
but far away, underneath, where reason doesn't reach,
in the unstoppable places. forget
the tree. turn off your thoughts, waft me away. let
                 there remain only life for your life,

Garden of Joy

we have mulched the earth with the salt of bodies

the cinnabar of the sky mixed with the oil in the
      puddles and the gold of the light on your lip

your body on the fluorescent grass of morning
the bedroom flooded by a phloem of light
and the vortex in the drapery, bright green over
                                        pale wood

drink this gold that has no way to die

From "Good Morals"

Incipit

exhumation of the amorous body. lacerating
the sheath of memory. exposing the gaps. astronomic vastness of
                               the beloved body. afterbirthing, in order
to expose the whole
of the amorous body
on the autopsy table. counting
the fissures of subsidence and distortions
of reality. the sagittal breast of the hard mother
originates behind the blind foramen
and is connected to the cerebral sickle. as love is let
thought be. the common melancholy of a fact: ending
by deliberate termination
of the heartbeat. residue discovered of the will
of another, resembling imitations of an idea
of the world. plastified slivers of reality
on the soft sublingual mucosa. right breast imperious. straddling
                               the mount. skimmed
rima of the mount. a droplet
of vital substance
still shines
in the light of the late summer
afternoon. left breast
petrous. terza rima
feeding into the jugular, gathered
in an outer tunic of amber skin
by means of perfectly pure blood. no decay. aggression of a lobe

of the thyroid. I will tend
to the snowfoam of your dreams
and the serene arch
of your diaphragm. the framework of nerves
in your lower limbs
vibrates like an elastic band. childlike smile. white as washbasin
                                      enamel. white as your heart
that trembled with acceleration and now rests in the sternal
                                                                             cavity
like a calcareous
shard. the concretion of my mute love in the golden disc
that you called abuse of power
has carved itself into the bitter caesura
of your lips, so beautiful. the common demonstration of a fact:
                                                                               loving
this vivid, impermeable being. tending
to its wonder and its ferocity. that is all there is on earth.

From "The Responsible Machine"

The Great Animal's Apocalypse

On the home front they unroll the dispatches under mining lamps
and the unknown travels through the country like barbed wire
                                                                              that hears
the beating of the soldiers' shovels, the enamel
of the mess kits against the tin
and yards of garlic. Maria, in our heads
there is such a shambles
the filth of beasts scrambling
underground, in our backs there is the buckling of mules
under the plebeian weight of the supplies. Give me your heart
Maria, so that your heart
weighs like earth in my hands
as I reach your side in danger. Maria, with your thoughts
that never stop thinking of me, even afterwards
hold me close, in my place
on the earth of names. Only you
know my name, Maria, because my name is at the rim
of your throat, white
as a drowned man in the canal
buried in your whiteness, resurfacing. Even afterwards,
tonight, when I am cinders, utter me Maria with your body.

Maria, the Apparitions

I dream of them, they call me, I see them
smiling and saying *come on
Maria, come and get us*, I hear
all this rustling of children and feel the stab of
        knowing they aren't in the house,
I see them in the house like ropes of fire with the fillings
                              of the dead
in the coagulations of blood
or they caress my lashes
wordless, for lack of themselves as language.

The World, Exposed

Love is a monkey's vigour.
The donkey's saintly eyes smeared by the view;
the quiet of the reservoirs, rusting.

The wind grinds the grass, the evening has
a shiny ultraviolet cup, a radiant latitude.

The sea and the afternoons,
the casing of a cicada nymph.

Give me the proof of your joy
inside the day's carcass
that you bite into to get to the light. The light...

Mosses Pave the Way for Spring

It was dark that evening—darkness being
rather sluggish and tranquil—and from it emerged
an old woman wearing a shawl and a long
black skirt. She said, if you want to save
your little girl, let her fast
days and nights; you can only
speak of the distance
between here and Paradise.
All that's left of the woman is the slip of the tongue
between my daughter and my life.

Inside the Crawling Month

The tremor in the lairs at dawn
takes on a new macerated majesty
to look into the beauty of the trees
in the mild days of late October.

The primary ultrasound of bells in the swooning hour
spangled with luminous knots.

We are an extreme race of azure blue
– new semblances erected
towers
receptions
detonated towers
that slowly collapse.

The rift of a body in time,
discharge of houses
in the imminence of a secular paradise.
In monstrances of snow
I found the faces
of soldiers, holy black wafers
– weighings
– hearts
of grubs
poor hearts sodden with matter.
A dark rumination under flakes of snow.

The Wind on the Sea Is Scaly Being Prone to Massacre

The wind – a squamous being that assaults us
bristling the bones of the hillside body
after the harvest;
a balance of placid verdigris, a lament, the
        fragrant cutting blades of underground
springs, the steadfast peace of coppery water,
                              victim of the heat
that declares its love for riddles and conditions us.

The volatile automotive host of iron and flesh
Is a nursery of concealed returns
water taken from the terraces and wheat fields
submerged
sanctuaries
drunk on wind and glory
of the solstice
bare and thundering
observatory full of euphoria and chill.

Said in Symbols

The beloved guide
lost in the snow
in a country in Northern
Europe. The language
of the passers-by is extremely
foreign. And so I mourn, not enough, in the dream
for my mother: a
snow I have never seen is her death and the house
is flooded and incurable, the pots and pans
are no longer hers, they're
different: not
mine, therefore, because I am the universal
heir and the house is a vast space
full of strangers
entering the body
that has in no way
come to an end inside those gleaming doors of sky blue
glasswork,
but is hospitable
alone.

Perhaps It Was the Age, the Circumstance

My hands are covered over by white stains like the bark
of a tree bowed by a strange sadness.

It's a sky-blue circle
the radiance of four-engined planes over the void
of the face set down stonewise
with a rifle alongside, the body like a great
seed cracked by the tree
in the swallowing of the earth.

We are intrigued by the position of bodies
when they are no longer responsible:
just as we are grub fished out
scooped up with scraps of newspaper
from the tracks – and we regret the body
towering
at the mercy of cloudy elements with rosaries
slipped into pockets
by mothers on an earth
to some degree clinging to the bone
in intermittent contact
with another huge
body and how sweet the agony of not being human beings.

Don't worry, watch your money, forgive
this earth and its language, with the joy
of an angel like a scale at the center of your breast that
cancels out the features and grass
slides from your palms.

The body is both springboard and rag
of the invisible
relationship
of proportionality between crime and punishment.
                                        Lingering in our memory
is this sorrow
between the excesses of the forest
the rapid midday ellipsis
of mineral magma
with clasped hands. The common soldier's shoe polish
marks the arsenal of nature
it's the sadness that he carries, the desperate
human weight of it on this frightening, mute earth.

I Did Not Move Ahead Just Barely Through the Water

The indifference of mimosas like a design of
                              swallows and sea
in the mullioned window of the underport – the steel
of the containers at the beginning of the air
lift over bodies like the bow of the new moon. I felt alone
maximally a man, that's how I wanted your body with no
                                                  resistance
like the bread broken by Christ.

The milestone experience of the pines
– the drills, the Spanish broom at the base of the pylon
isolated in the glass
and covered in lime.
The countryside touching the sky and the sea like infinite
gratitude
like your steps before sin.

Breathe in the air and the languishing particles,
for all eternity in brilliant explosions
of ammoniacal light:
        the toxic mold
        of Tutankhamon, the egg shape of the skull
                                  filled with boiling
        resin, golden rings at his knees where the
                                    bone began
        to react in the curve of the spine without ever
                                              resisting.

His voice was calm and truthful,
a love lavished out
the hemorrhagic reaction of a human tissue.
The bones show signs of healing now
they look
sick with gratitude.

More poetry published by SurVision Books in our New Poetics Series:

Noelle Kocot. Humanity
(New Poetics: USA)
ISBN 978-1-9995903-0-7

Ciaran O'Driscoll. The Speaking Trees
(New Poetics: Ireland)
ISBN 978-1-9995903-1-4

Elin O'Hara Slavick. Cameramouth
(New Poetics: USA)
ISBN 978-1-9995903-4-5

Anatoly Kudryavitsky. Stowaway
(New Poetics: Ireland)
ISBN 978-1-9995903-2-1

Sergey Biryukov. Transformations
Translated from Russian
(New Poetics: Russia)
ISBN 978-1-9995903-5-2

Our books are available to order via
http://survisionmagazine.com/books.htm

www.ingramcontent.com/pod-product-compliance
Lightning Source LLC
Chambersburg PA
CBHW061312040426
42444CB00010B/2606